Hi there!

Glad you picked up this book. This book is designed for anyone who'd like to learn how to write or recognize Chinese characters.

The truth is, there is a right and wrong way of writing each Chinese character: each stroke's starting point, direction and sequence matter. It's essential for learners to set up a good writing foundation.

We divided this book into 6 categories of sight words:
- Animals
- Family members
- Vehicles
- Foods
- Body parts
- Fruits

This book is meant for those who have learned how to write the easiest, most basic Chinese characters.

We choose these words because they are sight words that can be spotted often and in everyday lives. As we all know from research: repetition is key to learning anything.

Don't be intimidated with words that look a little more complex. We don't expect you or your child to memorize all characters, but tracing and writing them will help you to recognize those characters in the future. It's important to be exposed to more complex characters early.

This book shows you how to write each character the right way, with stroke by stroke examples in each character. Chinese characters are mostly written from left to right and top to bottom directions.

How to use this book:

- Read the word out loud by reading pinyin. If in doubt, many services online can help, from Google Translate to countless other apps
- Remember the meaning of the word - this should be easier with the help of illustrations on each page
- Trace the characters following the stroke order above with a marker, pencil or a pen
- Practice writing in the extra practice boxes provided in each page
- Feel free to complete the characters on the stroke order boxes to get more practice
- If still want to practice more, you can do so in a blank practice book

There are two kinds of Chinese characters: simplified and traditional. This book uses simplified Chinese characters (mainly used in mainland China and Singapore) and pinyin romanization.

I'm a grandfather passionate about all things Chinese and with my daughter, I created this book after seeing how hard it is for Mia, my 5 year old granddaughter to learn to write Chinese.

She would write the characters with wrong directions and stroke sequences. This book is designed for learners like her.

I hope you'll find this book useful in your journey, too.

牛

Niú

Cow

牛 ノ ㇒ ㇓ 牛

牛 牛 牛 牛 牛

马

Mǎ

Horse

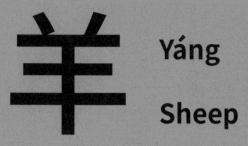

Yáng

Sheep

猫

Māo

Cat

猫	⺈	犭	犭	犭
犭	犭	犭	犭	猫
猫	猫	猫	猫	猫
猫	猫			

鸟

Niǎo

Bird

鸟	′	勹	勺	鸟
鸟	鸟	鸟	鸟	鸟
鸟				

猪 Zhū

Pig

猪	ノ	丿	犭
犭	犭	犭	犭	猪
猪	猪	猪	猪	猪
猪	猪		

狗

Gǒu

Dog

狗	ノ	犭	犭
犭	狗	狗	狗
狗	狗	狗	狗

鱼

Yú

Fish

鱼	ノ	ク	各	各
各	角	鱼	鱼	鱼
鱼	鱼	鱼	鱼	

老虎

Lǎo hǔ

Tiger

老	一	十	土	少
少	老	老	老	老
老	老			

老虎 Lǎo hǔ
Tiger

虎	丨	卜	上	卢
卢	卢	虎	虎	虎
虎	虎	虎	虎	

兔子

Tù zǐ

Rabbit

兔子

Tù zǐ

Rabbit

子 𠃌 了 子 子

子 子 子 子

我

Wǒ

Me

我	丿	二	干	手
我	我	我	我	我
我	我	我		

爸爸

Bà ba

Father

爸	⺁	ハ	少	父
爷	爷	爸	爸	爸
爸	爸	爸	爸	

妈妈

Mā mā

Mother

妈	く	ㄑ	女	女ㄱ
妈	妈	妈	妈	妈
妈	妈			

姐姐

Jiě jiě

Elder sister

姐 く ㄑ 女 如

如 如 姐 姐 姐

姐 姐 姐 姐

哥哥

Gē gē

Elder brother

弟弟

Dì dì

Younger brother

弟　、　丷　丷　丷

丷　弟　弟　弟　弟

弟　弟　弟

妹妹

Mèi mei

Younger sister

爷爷

Yé yé

Paternal
Grandfather

爷

丶 八 ⺈ 父

爸 爷 爷 爷 爷

爷 爷

奶奶

Nǎi nai

Grandmother

奶	㇉	㇉	女	奶
奶	奶	奶	奶	奶
奶				

公公

Gōng gong

Grandfather

公 ノ 八 公 公

婆婆

Pó po

Grandmother

婆	`	` `	氵	氵
氵	汴	沙	波	波
婆	婆	婆	婆	婆
婆	婆			

伯伯

Bó bo

Father's elder brother

伯 ノ イ イ´ 伊

伈 伯 伯 伯 伯

伯 伯 伯

叔叔

Shū shu

Father's younger brother

叔　丶　上　上　丄

丰　朩　叔　叔　叔

叔　叔　叔　叔

姑姑

Gū gū

Father's sister

姑　ㄑ　ㄑ　ㄑ　女

女　奴　姑　姑　姑

姑　姑　姑　姑

阿姨

Ā yí

Mother's sister

阿	阝	阝	阝
阝	阝	阿	阿
阿	阿	阿	

姨

yí
Mother's sister

姨　㇏　ㄑ　女　女⁻

女⁻　女⁻　姤　姨　姨

姨　姨　姨　姨　姨

舅舅

Jiù jiu

Mother's brother

舅	丿	丿	彳	彳
彳	臼	臼	臼	臼
臼	畠	畠	舅	舅
舅	舅	舅	舅	

婶婶

Wife of father's younger brother

婶 く ㄠ 女 女

女 疒 疒 妒 婡

婡 婶 婶 婶 婶

婶 婶

车

Chē

Car

车　一　七　七　车

车　车　车　车　车

船

Chuán

Boat

船	´	㇒	刀	刀
舟	舟	舟	舯	舡
船	船	船	船	船
船	船			

火车

Huǒ chē

Train

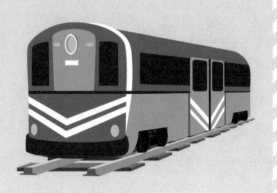

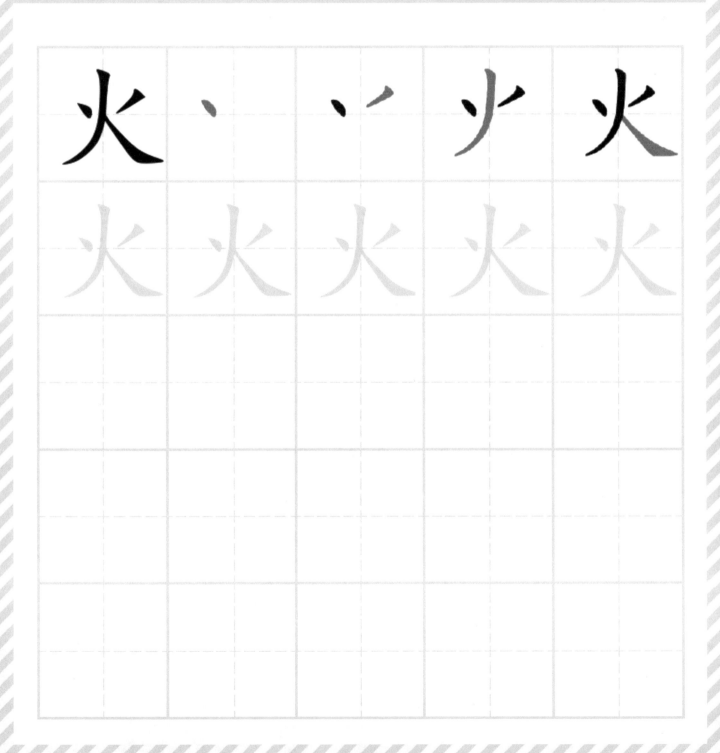

火车 **Huǒ chē**

Train

车 一 仁 仨 车

车 车 车 车 车

飞机

Fēi jī

Airplane

飞机

Fēi jī

Airplane

机	一	十	才	木
木	机	机	机	机
机	机			

卡车

Kǎ chē

Truck

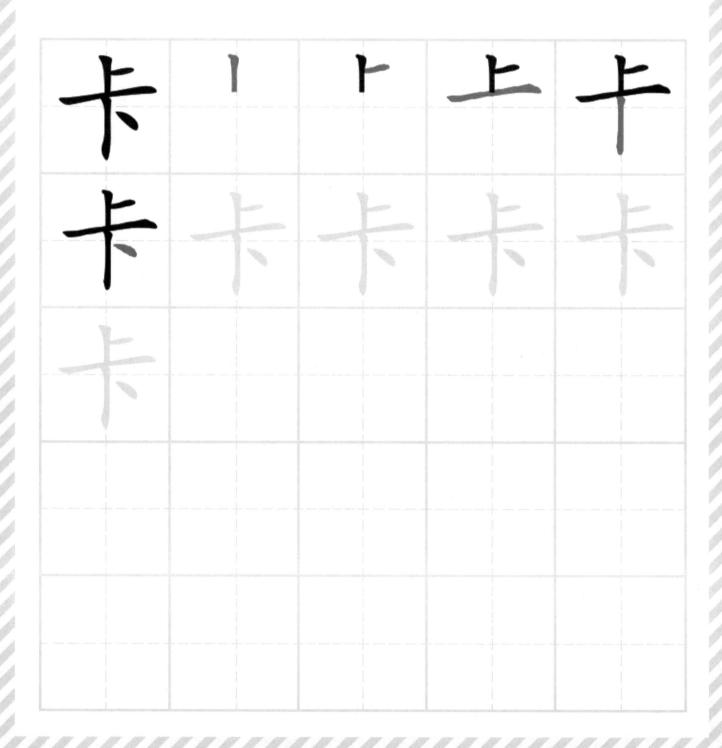

卡车 Kǎ chē

Truck

车　一　七　七　车

车　车　车　车　车

电车

Diàn chē

Tram

电	丶	冂	冂	日
电	电	电	电	电
电				

电车 **Diàn chē**
Tram

车　　一　　七　　丰　　车

校车

Xiào chē

School bus

校	一	十	才	木
术	杧	杧	柠	柠
校	校	校	校	校
校				

校**车** Xiào chē
School bus

车	一	七	乍	车
车	车	车	车	车

高铁

High-speed train

高	﹨	一	亠	亠
亠	宀	高	高	高
高	高	高	高	高
高				

高铁 Gāo tiě

High-speed train

铁 丿 ㇏ ㇏ 乍

乍 牟 钅 钅 铁

铁 铁 铁 铁 铁

铁

坦克 Tǎn kè

Tank

坦	一	十	坩
坩	坦	坦	坦
坦	坦	坦	坦

坦克 **Tǎn kè**
Tank

克	一	十	古	古
古	声	克	克	克
克	克	克		

巴士

Bā shì

Bus

巴　㇖　㇕　卫　巴

巴　巴　巴　巴　巴

 士 **Bā shì**

Bus

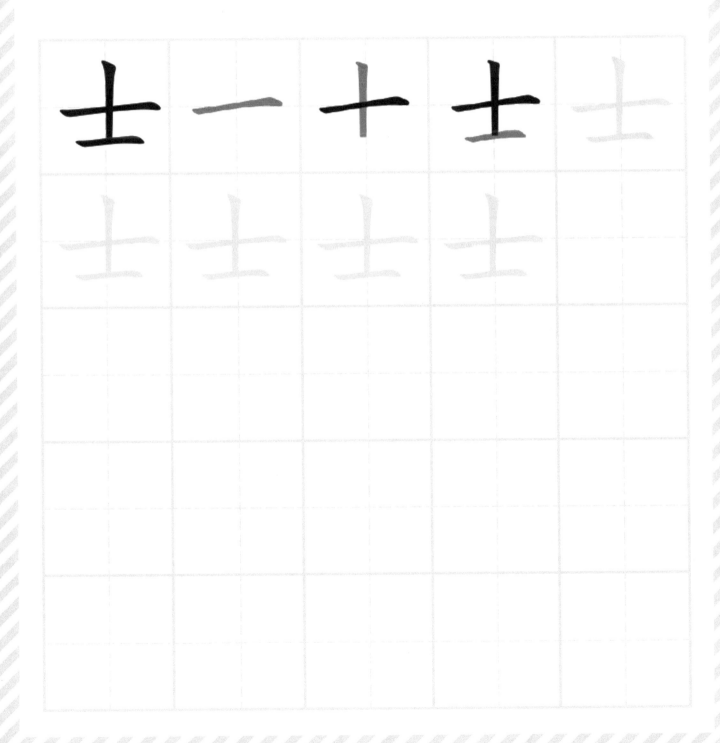

肉

Ròu

Meat

肉	丨	冂	内	内
肉	肉	肉	肉	肉
肉	肉			

菜

Cài

Vegetable

菜	一	十	艹	艹
艹	艻	芯	苙	苹
苹	菜	菜	菜	菜
菜	菜			

茶

Chá

Tea

茶	一	十	艹	艼
艿	芡	芐	苶	茶
茶	茶	茶	茶	茶

汤

Tāng

Soup

汤	、	㇇	氵	汋
汤	汤	汤	汤	汤
汤	汤			

鸡蛋

Jī dàn

Egg

鸡	フ	ヌ	ヌ′	邓
邓	鸡	鸡	鸡	鸡
鸡	鸡	鸡		

鸡蛋

Jī dàn

Egg

蛋	一	下	下	严
疋	疋	疋	蛋	蛋
蛋	蛋	蛋	蛋	蛋
蛋	蛋			

牛扒

Niú bā

Steak

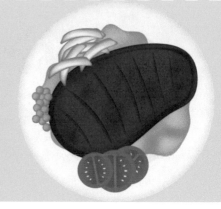

牛　ノ　ト　卜　牛

牛　牛　牛　牛　牛

牛扒 Niú bā
Steak

扒	一	十	扌	扌
扒	扒	扒	扒	扒
扒				

面包

Miàn bāo

Bread

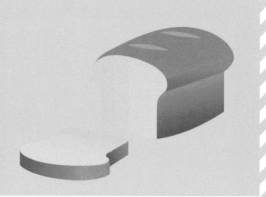

面	一	丆	丆	丙
而	而	而	而	面
面	面	面	面	面

面包 Miàn bāo

Bread

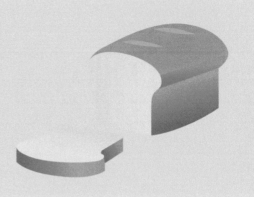

包	╱	勹	勺	勺
包	包	包	包	包
包				

白饭

Bái fàn

Rice

白	ノ	亻	白	白
白	白	白	白	白
白				

白饭

Bái fàn

Rice

饭 丿 𠂉 饣 饣

饣 饭 饭 饭 饭

饭 饭 饭

起司

Qǐ sī

Cheese

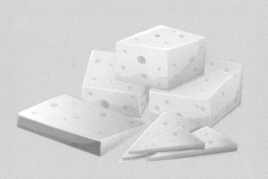

起	一	十	土	丰
丰	丰	走	起	起
起	起	起	起	起
起				

起司

Qǐ sī

Cheese

司	丁	刁	刁	司
司	司	司	司	司
司				

牛奶

Niú nǎi

Milk

牛　ノ　ㇷ　䒑　牛

牛　牛　牛　牛　牛

牛奶

Niú nǎi

Milk

奶	く	々	女	奶
奶	奶	奶	奶	奶
奶				

水果

Shuǐ guǒ

Fruit

水	亅	刁	水	水
水	水	水	水	水

水果 Shuǐ guǒ
Fruit

果	丶	冂	冂	日
旦	早	甲	果	果
果	果	果	果	

头

Tóu

Head

头	丶	丷	丷一	头
头	头	头	头	头
头				

手

Shǒu

Hand

手	一	二	三	手
手	手	手	手	手

脚

Jiǎo

Foot

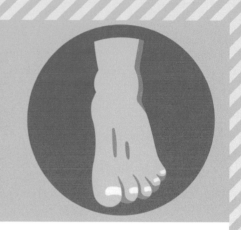

脚	ノ	刀	月	月
月	肝	肤	胠	胠
胠	脚	脚	脚	脚
脚	脚			

舌

Shé

Tongue

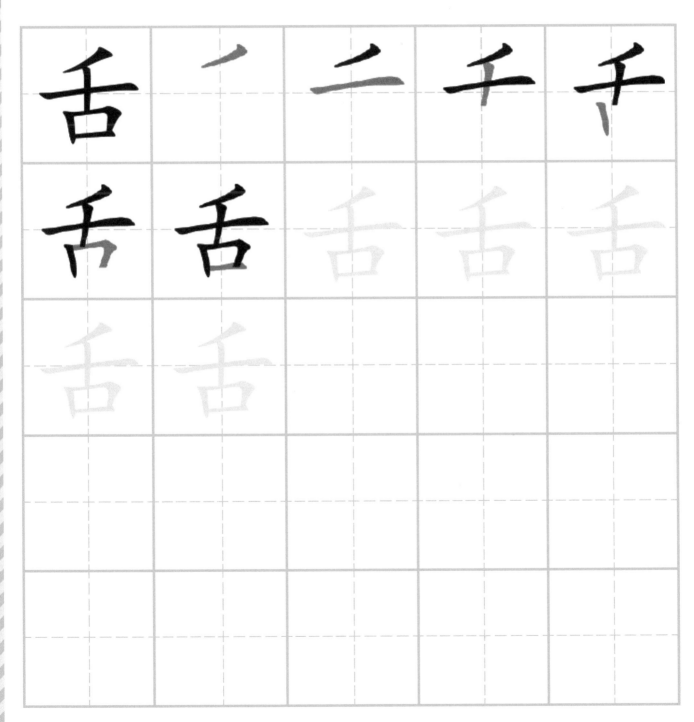

头发

Tóu fǎ

Hair

头	丶	丷	丷	头
头	头	头	头	头
头				

头发 Tóu fǎ
Hair

发	㇇	㇒	𠂇	发
发	发	发	发	发
发				

牙齿

Yá chǐ

Teeth

牙　一　二　牙　牙

牙　牙　牙　牙　牙

牙齿

Yá chǐ

Teeth

齿

丨	卜	止	止
步	步	齿	齿

手指

Shǒu zhǐ

Finger

手	一	二	三	手
手	手	手	手	手

手指

指	一	丁	扌
扌	扗	指	指	指
指	指	指	指	指

耳朵 Ěr duǒ

Ear

耳	一	厂	丌	丌
丌	耳	耳	耳	耳
耳	耳			

耳朵

Ěr duǒ

Ear

朵	丿	几	几	乒
乒	朵	朵	朵	朵
朵	朵			

眼睛 Yǎn jīng

Eye

眼	丨	冂	月	月
目	目	目	目	眼
眼	眼	眼	眼	眼
眼	眼			

眼睛 Yǎn jīng

Eye

睛	丨	冂	月	月
目	目一	目二	目キ	睛
睛	睛	睛	睛	睛
睛	睛	睛	睛	

鼻子 Bí zi

Nose

鼻	⟍	⟍	𠂊	白
白	白	白	臭	臭
臭	畠	鼻	鼻	鼻
鼻	鼻	鼻	鼻	鼻

鼻子

Bí zi

Nose

嘴巴

Zuǐ bā

Mouth

嘴	丨	口	口丿	口卜
口卜	口卜	呰	呰一	呰比
呰比	嘴比	嘴	嘴	嘴
嘴	嘴	嘴	嘴	嘴
嘴	嘴			

嘴巴 Zuǐ bā
Mouth

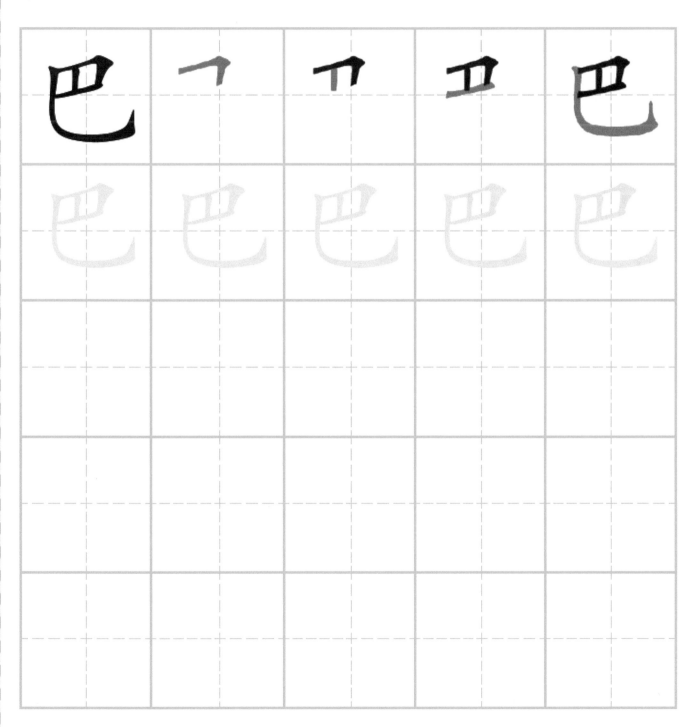

西瓜

Xī guā

Watermelon

西	一	一	一	丙
丙	西	西	西	西
西	西			

西瓜

Xī guā

Watermelon

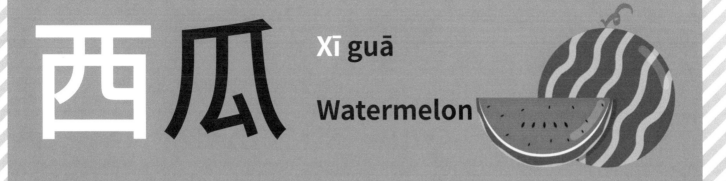

瓜	一	厂	瓜	瓜
瓜	瓜	瓜	瓜	瓜
瓜				

Mù guā

Papaya

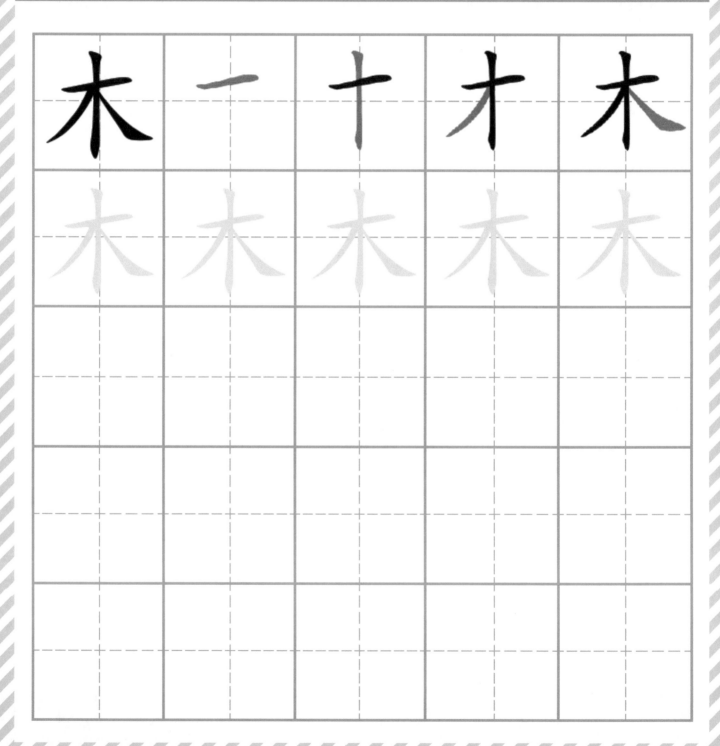

木瓜

Mù guā

Papaya

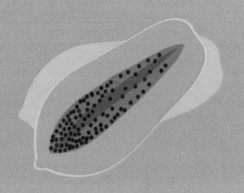

瓜	一	厂	厂	瓜
瓜	瓜	瓜	瓜	瓜
瓜				

梨子

Lí zi

Pear

梨	一	二	千	禾
禾	利	利	利	利
梨	梨	梨	梨	梨
梨	梨			

梨子

Lí zi

Pear

子　了　了　子　子

子　子　子　子

苹果

Píng guǒ

Apple

苹	一	十	艹	芢
芢	芣	苹	苹	苹
苹	苹	苹	苹	

苹果

Píng guǒ

Apple

果	丶	冂	冃	日
旦	早	甲	果	果
果	果	果	果	

芒果

Máng guǒ

Mango

芒	一	十	艹	艹
艾	芒	芒	芒	芒
芒	芒			

芒果

果	丶	冂	冂	曰
旦	早	畢	果	果
果	果	果	果	

香蕉

Xiāng jiāo

Banana

香	一	二	千	千
禾	禾	香	香	香
香	香	香	香	香

香蕉

Xiāng jiāo

Banana

蕉	一	一	艹	艹
艹	艿	艿	荐	荐
荐	萑	萑	萑	蕉
蕉	蕉	蕉	蕉	蕉
蕉				

柚子

Yòu zi

Grapefruit

柚	一	十	才
木	杧	朷	柚	柚
柚	柚	柚	柚	柚

柚子

Yòu zi

Grapefruit

桃子

Táo zi

Peach

桃	一	十	才	才
杧	杧	杧	枕	桃
桃	桃	桃	桃	桃

桃子

Táo zi

Peach

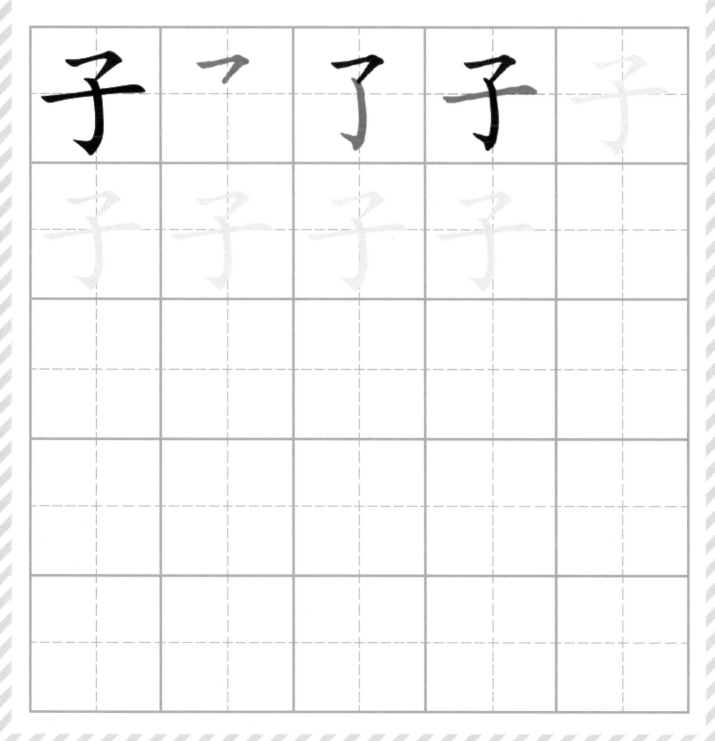

Made in the USA
Columbia, SC
09 October 2024

44006156R00059